My Little Fountain of Youth Book

2

My Little Fountain of Youth Book

√ *adds years to your life, and life to your years*

√ *gives you 365 ways to look, feel, and be younger every day*

√ *finds fast, easy anti-aging foods, right in your own kitchen*

√ *boosts your brain power and keeps you thinking young*

√ *sparks up your love life and rekindles that first love feeling*

√ *shows you how to fight wrinkles, middle-age spread, and gravity*

Important Please Read Carefully

The information about aging and anti-aging is both confusing and exciting.

Many experts now agree that the aging process may be influenced by certain lifestyle choices--especially diet and nutrition, exercise, and stress management. Because my research comes from many diverse sources, it merely reflects my own view and is accurate to the best of my knowledge.

I do not directly or indirectly dispense medical advice or prescribe or offer any of these suggestions as forms of treatment without medical approval. The ideas, information, and suggestions in this book are not intended to substitute for the services of a physician. This book is a reference guide only, not a manual for self-treatment.

It is only my intention to offer this information to be used in conjunction with your own physician. Always see your own doctor before embarking on any diet, exercise or other lifestyle and health-related course.

Fountain of Youth Group, Inc.
830-13 A1A North
Ponte Vedra Beach, FL 32082

ISBN Number 0963515020
Printed in the United States of America
1 2 3 4 5 6 7 8 9 10

To all of us
from
"thirty-something"
to
a "hundred-and-something"
and
counting....

"Old age must be resisted..."

Cicero

"I have never admitted that I
am
more than twenty-nine or thirty at
the most.
Twenty-nine when there are pink
shades,
thirty when there are not."

Oscar Wilde

"We turn not older with years,
but newer every day."

Emily Dickinson

Contents

My Thank You Page

Every book I've ever read had a special page in the front for thanking people. I used to skip that page most of the time. But having written a book myself, I don't think I'll ever skip over the thank you page again. And so, on my thank you page, I would like to tell those special people who were there for me, how much I appreciate their help and support.

First as always, my son Mark, who believes in me as much as I believe in him. Marge who has always called me #1. Also, Eva, Bonnie, Martha, Lillian, David, Sylvia, Barbara, Tom, Stephanie, Mary, Ken, and most especially Pam.

I would also like to thank all those scientists, who have dedicated their lives to the belief that we can indeed turn back the hands of time and restore youth to our body, mind and spirit.

Edita Says...

I have presented all the information here in as true and as accurate a form as I could. Everything is based on the latest scientific information. I spent hundreds of hours researching, reading, compiling and analyzing countless papers, scientific articles and studies.

All this research and effort has been for one purpose, and one purpose only--to provide you with a single, simplified, friendly and practical guide to looking, feeling and being as young as you can, for as long as you can.

Don't let the size or simplicity fool you. Less, in this case is very much more. For the first time you have in your hands the one book that can be used as your personal anti-aging road map. Start on your journey with a light heart, because it will take you and the ones you love and care about to better health and a longer life.

Edita Kaye
1996

Getting Started

My Little Fountain Of Youth Book

1

How old would you be if you didn't know how old you were?

Go ahead. Be it. Act it. Live it.

2

The journey to youth, like all journeys, begins with the first step. So go ahead. Take it.

3

Surround yourself with people that make you feel young.

4

Stop worrying. Nothing ages you faster than climbing the mountain, **before** you get to it.

5

Want an instant youth pill?
Just lie about your age.

6

If you're not dead, you're not too old.

7

Celebrate something.

> Celebrate Monday
> Celebrate Tuesday
> Celebrate Spring
> Celebrate Rain
>
> Celebrate Being Alive
>
> Celebrate Yourself...Getting Younger

8

Get with the vocabulary

Anti-aging
Longevity
Life Extension
Rejuventation

De-Aging
Retro-Age
The Best Years
Youthfulness

9

Live young one day at a time.

If you can't do that, then try living young one hour at a time...and work your way up.

10

Make love.

11

Make love again.

12

Twice is enough, unless you are with a much younger lover, then go right ahead.

13

Think positive.
If you were born in ancient Greece your life expectancy would have been 22.

14

If you're alive in the 1990s your lifespan potential is 115. Go for it!

15

Plan the best party for New Year's Eve 2000. Start right now.

16

You're never too old.....

• George Burns won his first Oscar at eighty.

• George Bernard Shaw was ninety-four when his first play was produced.

• Grandma Moses didn't start painting until she was eighty and then finished 1500 pictures.

• Michaelangelo painted the Sistine Chapel when he was seventy-one.

17

Volunteer in a nursing home.
Volunteer in a kindergarten.

Do them both on the same day.

Go ahead. You'll see what I mean.

18

Find one day a week to rest...really rest both your body and your mind.

God did. So should you.

19

Lighten up. Have some fun....

Blow up a balloon
Play with an electric train
Swing on a swing
Toss a ball
Color a picture with crayons

These activities should be done regularly, with or without a kid.

20

Become a longevity "groupie."

21

Go with the flow.

22

Get rural.

City people just don't live as long as
 country folk...

23

"The Four Empties," or The Zen Answer To A
Long Life

Empty mind	=	no worry
Empty stomach	=	moderation
Empty kitchen	=	buy often, buy fresh
Empty room	=	avoid life clutter

24

Stop getting older. Start getting better.

25

What's Hot	What's Not
Hair color	Grey
Walking	Couch potatoes
Dental implants	False teeth glue
Sunscreen	Tanned wrinkles
Multiple careers	Retirement
Veggies	Everything else

26

Fifty is fine to join the AARP.
Call 202-434-2277.

Give a gift membership to someone you love.

Give a gift membership to someone you like.

27

Start your own anti-aging library.

Ageless Body, Timeless Mind, by Deepak Chopra.

Eat Away Illness: How To Age-Proof Your Body With Antioxidant Foods by Carlson Wade.

How A Man Ages: Growing Older--What To Expect And What You Can Do About It by Curtis Pesman (Same for women).

How To Live Longer And Feel Better by Linus Pauling.

28

Celebrate your birthday every two years. Not as dumb as it sounds. Better than being 29 or 39 for the tenth time!

You may miss out on some presents, but it'll be worth it.

29

Get a pet.

30

No home should be without....

√ Plenty of sunscreen.

√ UV coated sunglasses.

√ A healthy cookbook.

√ A basket for steaming vegetables.

√ A juicer.

√ A hot air popcorn popper.

√ A water pik.

√ A water cooler.

√ Fresh vitamins.

31

Get political.

Lobby for more research dollars to go into studies on nutrition, prevention, and longevity.

Start with your congressman and senator.

32

Hug a kid.
Hug your mate.
Hug a teddy bear.

Hug yourself.

33

Write a personal resume for yourself for after you retire.

Remember, you may have fifty or more years to fill.

34

Start an anti-aging support group.

35

Collect "You're Never Too Old Stories."

36

Keep your environment clean.

The Surgeon General in his report, *Healthy People*, says, "There is virtually no major chronic disease to which environmental factors do not contribute, directly or indirectly."

37

Listen to, sing, or hum show tunes, patriotic songs, good old spirituals...anything that gets your toes to tappin'...and do it often!

38

Start taking care of yourself, **before** you get older.

39

Give yourself the most precious gift of all--time.

Cater a meal, even if it's just for the family.

Hire a house cleaner.

Send the laundry out, all the laundry, not just the shirts.

Get a babysitter even when you aren't going out.

Shop by phone.

Get up an hour earlier.

Go to bed an hour later.

40

Bored?

Boring is aging. Get an interest. Get a life.

41

Jake: "Say, Doc, what do you think is wrong with my right knee?"

Doc: "Well, Jake, you've got to remember that your knee is 85 years old."

Jake: "Yeah, but so's my left knee, and it's fine."

42

Call an old friend. Reminisce.

43

Make a new friend. Start some memories.

44

Surround yourself with beauty.

Beautiful things

Beautiful thoughts

45

More "you're never too old" inspirations...

• Casey Stengel didn't retire from the Mets until he was seventy five.

• Winston Churchill became Prime Minister of England at sixty-five.

• Henry Ford didn't get anything going until he was past forty.

• Neither did Abraham Lincoln.

46

Write down at least one anti-aging thing a day on your to-do list. Then do it.

47

Fall in love.

48

Fall in love again.

49

Get involved. Go to meetings. Learn something.

Annual Meeting of the American Aging
Association
610-874-7550

50

Take five years off your age.

51

Add five years to your kids' ages.

52

Denial works.

"I refuse to admit I'm more than fifty-two, even if that does make my sons illegitimate." *Lady Astor*

53

Do you act older than you really are?

Before you shake your head ask someone who loves you. Believe their answer.

54

Invest in a copy of *The Oxford Book of Ages* edited by Anthony and Sally Sampson...read a quote or two to get your youth juices flowing.

55

Visualize yourself young. Need help? Write some of your favorite tips from *My Little Fountain Of Youth Book* on stick-ums. Now put them...

...on your fridge (better than ice-cream)

...on your make-up or shaving mirror (smile)

...in your wallet (almost as good as cash)

...on your dashboard

...on your desk

...in an envelope and mail one to yourself

...on your pillow (fewer calories than a mint)

56

You are never too old to...

o Go on a picnic

o Stop and smell the roses

o Smile

o Listen to wonderful music

o Play with a kid

o Have a dream

57

Start an anti-aging investment portfolio...Look into some of these:

A swimming pool where you can do laps and water exercises.

Investment: $7,000 to $10,000.

A healthclub membership.

Investment: $1,000

Personal treadmill, stair-climber, or cross-country machine.

Investment: $2,000

Personal trainer three times per week.

Investment: $150

A good juicer.

Investment: $200

58

Give a copy of this book to a friend or loved one you would like to keep around for a very long time.

59

Declare tomorrow "Fountain of Youth" Day.

60

Don't let aging become a self-fulfilling prophesy.

My Little Fountain Of Youth Book

Good Health is Long Life

My Little Fountain Of Youth Book

61

Always get a second opinion.

62

The Surgeon General reports that two-thirds of the ailments encountered before age 65 are preventable.

The ability to lengthen your life depends first on your capacity not to shorten it.

63

Slow down.

Walk slower	Eat slower
Drive slower	Breathe slower

Stop and smell the flowers...hay fever is no excuse!!!

64

Live abroad.

In Japan men live to 74.8, women to 80.7
In Switzerland men live to 73.8, women to 80.8
In Iceland men live to 73.4, women to 80.6
In the USA men live to 70.9, women to 78.4

65

Teach your kids to say "no" to drugs.

66

Say "no" to drugs yourself.

67

"What does your doctor say about your drinking and smoking cigars?"
"My doctor's dead." *George Burns*

68

Are you going deaf?

Rub your thumb and forefinger together near your ear. If you can't hear the sound get your hearing checked out.

National Information Center on Deafness
Washington, D.C.

Food and Drug Administration
Office of Consumer Affairs/Hearing Information
Rockville, MD.

69

Sleepless in Seattle, or anywhere else in the country? Try these do-it-yourself sleep rejuvenating tips from the Orient.

o Press and massage the little hollows just below
    your ankles inside and outside your leg.
o Rub the spot just above your nose between your
    eyes.

70

No home should be without a copy of...

The PDR Family Guide to Prescription Drugs.
Available from Medical Economics
1-800-232-7379.

71

Imagine if you picked up the paper and read that three 747s crashed yesterday, killing 1,000 people. Horrible news, right? Guess what? That's how many people die every single day from smoking. If you smoke, quit. If you know someone who smokes, get them to quit.

72

Take control of your own health. Start by keeping your own medical records. In a small notebook record...

o your family medical history (both sides)
o childhood diseases
o allergies (food and drug)
o surgeries with dates
o pregnancies
o medications and prescriptions (don't forget
      eyeglasses)
o last weight, blood pressure, cholesterol reading
o accidents
o any time you were hospitalized, and why
o innoculations
o date of last chest x-ray
o any new stressors in your life

73

Getting younger is 90% maintenance and only 10% genes.

Grandparents who lived long and were healthy are just a bonus, adding about 3 years to your possible lifespan. But by living a healthy life, you can add dozens more and beat your genetic odds.

74

Avoid "wet T-shirt" contests, unless they are indoors.

If your T-shirt gets wet, its SPF goes way down, giving you less protection from the sun.

75

Is your job making you older by the day?
Stay safe. Stay healthy. Stay stress-free.

76

Learn CPR and the Heimlich Maneuver.

77

Half the battle in getting younger is finding the right doctor. Try calling the...

American College for the Advancement of Medicine
714-583-7666

National Center for Homeopathy
703-548-7790

National Women's Health Network
202-347-1140

78

Don't forget to protect your hands with sunscreen.

15 SPF is good. 30 SPF is better.

79

Never drink and drive.

Never drive with a drunk.

80

Cleaning house may be killing you in more ways than one. Switch to natural cleaning products.

Debra Lynn Dadd tells you how in her book, *Nontoxic and Natural: How to Avoid Dangerous Everyday Products and Buy or Make Safe Ones.*

81

"Age does not depend upon years, but upon temperament and health. Some men are born old, and some never grow so."   *Tryon Edwards*

82

Need surgery?

Look into lasers.

Available for many procedures. Recovery time is faster. Less stress on the body. Fewer risks.

83

If you have problems with your teeth or gums, don't blame aging...blame poor dental habits.

o find a good dentist.

o brush and floss regularly after
   meals.

o chew sugar-free gum to keep saliva
   flowing.

o look into the new cosmetic possibilities
   for a youthful smile.

84

Look after your bones.
Osteoporosis is the fourth leading cause of death
for women.

"Stand Up To Osteoporosis" is a free pamphlet
available from the National Osteoporosis
Foundation 1-800-223-9994.

Cook the lowfat calcium-rich way with
*Bone Builders™The Complete Lowfat Cookbook
Plus Calcium Heath Guide,* by Edita Kaye and
published by Warner Books.

85

Dial 1-800-FOR-HEALTH.

You'll get a booklet that lists over 350 health
agencies and their toll-free numbers.

86

If your feet hurt, it shows on your face. Take off a few years fast.

Treat your feet to...

o a pedicure.

o comfortable shoes.

o a soft pair of slippers.

o a soak in bath oil or Epsom salts.

o a workout...stand with your feet flat on the floor and curl your toes under. Repeat 10 times.

o and don't forget the plain vanilla treatment--put your feet up.

87

Practice safe sex--always. Better yet, be faithful and true.

88

"While others may argue about whether the world ends with a bang or a whimper, I just want to make sure mine doesn't end with a whine."

Barbara Gordon, Writer.

89

Give your brain a break.

Switch to roll-on deodorants.

Why?

Almost all spray antiperspirants contain aluminum. Aluminum is found in large amounts in the brains of Alzheimer's patients.

Also, our nose doesn't have the world's greatest filtering system. So don't breathe aluminum if you can avoid it.

Give your brain a break.

90

Have A Safe Flight.

Don't fly in snow or freezing rain.

Get a seat close to an exit.

Count off the seat backs between you
and an exit.

Count off the seat backs between you
and an alternative exit.

Fly in off-peak hours.

Avoid high air traffic airports.

Check under your seat to make sure your
life vest is there. (People do take
them for souvenirs... no kidding)

91

Clean out your insides.

Try a colonic. You'll live longer, feel better, and be healthier with no toxins gumming up the works.

Before you go "yuck" contact the National Colon Therapists' Association in Washington.

92

Get regular check-ups.

93

Smokers are losers: If you smoke...

1-9 cigarettes per day, take 4.6 years off your life.
10-19 per day, take 5.5 years off your life.
20-39 per day, take 6.1 years off your life.
40 to 60 per day, take 8.1 years off your life.

More than three packs per day.....you haven't got a life!

94

Do you live in Wrinkle Town, U.S.A.?

The more exposure you have to sunlight without protection, the greater your chances of developing wrinkles, lines, or skin cancer. The stronger the sun in your community the more you need protection.

95

Take a nap.

96

Take another nap.

97

Want to keep your voice young?

- o Keep your lungs in top shape.

- o Stop smoking.

- o Drink water or sip herbal tea to keep vocal cords moist.

- o Hum for a few minutes a day. It's good exercise.

98

Watch out for glare...it can burn too.

Snow reflects up to 80% of the sun's rays, doubling their strength.

Sand reflects up to 17% of the sun's rays...

Water reflects up to 10% of the sun's rays...

99

Wear hats with a brim all around...ears age too.

Wear shades with wrap-around frames...
eyes age too.

100

Is your blood pressure aging you, prematurely?
Get it down.

Age	BP	Added Life Expectancy	
		Men	Women
45	120/80	32	37
	130/90	29	35.5
	140/90	26	32
	150/100	20.5	28.5
55	120/80	23.5	27.5
	130/90	22.5	27
	140/95	19.5	24.5
	150/100	17.5	23.5

101

Add years to your life.

Attend the annual meeting of the
Foundation for the Advancement of
Innovative Medicine. Call 914-368-9797.

102

Know where to get help when you need it.

Alzheimer's Disease Association 1-800-621-0379

Arthritis Foundation 404-872-7100

American Cancer Society 212-856-8700

American Heart Association 1-800-242-1793

American Diabetes Association 703-549-1500

American Lung Association 212-315-8700

103

Anti-aging on a budget try...

> A humungous salad.
> A good pair of walking shoes.
> Sunscreen.
> A big smile on your face.

104

Anti-aging first class all the way

> Same as 103, plus...
> A month in a top spa.
> Around the world on the Q.E.II.
> Your own personal gym...with trainer.
> Plastic surgery from the bottom up.

105

Send a copy of this book to your doctor, shrink, dermatologist, ophthalmologist, chiropractor, etc.

My Little Fountain Of Youth Book

The Fountain of Youth is in Your Kitchen

My Little Fountain Of Youth Book

106

Looking for the Fountain of Youth? Look no further than your own kitchen.

Open your fridge and eat something orange, green, red, or yellow.

Open your fridge and drink something orange, white or sparkling and clear.

107

Yes, you **can** eat years away. How?

With these anti-aging nutrients:

Vitamin C, Vitamin E, Beta-carotene & Calcium

Vitamin C	1,000 mg./day--food is best.
Vitamin E	400 I.U./day--food is best.
Beta-carotene	20,000 I.U./day--food is best.
Calcium	1,000 mg./day--food is best.

108

Review your diet with a good nutritionist at least once a year.

- Write down everything you eat...don't cheat.
- Cut both the fat and the calories.
- Add calcium every day.
- Eat fresh, natural foods.

109

Questions to ask your doctor: Did you study nutrition? Do you believe good nutrition can make me younger? Healthier? Do you read current anti-aging literature?

If the answer to any one of these questions is **NO**. Find a doctor who believes in nutrition to be your anti-aging specialist.Try.....

The Alliance for Alternative Medicine
    503-926-4678
Academy of Orthomolecular Medicine
    416-733-2117
American Association of Naturopathic Physicians
    206-323-7610

110

Shop your local health food store as often as you shop in your supermarket.

111

Shop your local farmer's markets as often, or more often, than you shop in your local supermarket.

112

Garnish. Garnish. Garnish.

Not only will your plate look full and yummy, but munching all that healthy, fresh, irresistible garnish will add 'mucho' anti-aging nutrients to your diet.

Try these anti-aging garnishes:
- o parsley
- o basil
- o mint
- o slivers of red and green peppers

113

From the man who hates broccoli.

What does former President Bush call carrots?
You guessed it. "Orange broccoli."

114

Keep your supplements fresh.
Replace them every 6 months.

115

Take anti-oxidant vitamins (vitamin C and E)
right after meals. They will detoxify aging foods
that throw off damaging free radicals through the
digestive process.

116

Chinese takeout? Order bird's nest soup.
The Chinese for centuries have sworn by its
youth-giving properties.

117

Move that fat. Increase the amount of fiber in your diet and get that fat through and out of your system, fast.

118

How does **your** fridge stack up? Best bets for longevity...

o skim milk
o low fat yogurt
o whole wheat bread
o olive oil
o fresh veggies
o low fat cottage cheese
o bottled water
o fresh herbs

o fresh pasta
o sprouts
o fresh fruit
o lowfat dressings
o flaxseed oil
o wheat germ
o tofu
o garlic

119

Stop committing "sweet suicide".
Get rid of the sugar.

120

The Japanese do it again!

Japanese persimmons have three times the vitamin C and more fiber than American citrus fruit. Learn how to grow your own.

Contact U.S. Dept. of Agriculture, P.O. Box 87, 111 New Bunbar Rd., Buroa, GA 31008.

121

For every "bad" thing you eat (and you know what those are)....eat one "good" thing.

122

Learn to brew & drink herbal teas.

123

Less is more.
All things in moderation.

Especially food.

124

The best anti-aging foods:

Asparagus	Garlic
Cereal	Oat Bran
Papaya	Parsley
Salmon	Sardines
Squash	Basil
Yams	Yogurt
Carrots	Broccoli
Cantaloupe	Romaine
Cauliflower	Celery

125

Give a copy of this book to your favorite cook.

126

Can't get those anti-aging 8 to 10 glasses of
water down?

Try......
- o flavoring with vanilla or a squeeze of
  fresh juice
- o herbal teas...hot or cold
- o sucking on ice cubes
- o sipping designer water...plain or bubbly
- o water-logged foods, like melon and
  lettuce
- o using your very best champagne flute

127

Less is more say scientists.

The National Institutes of Health studies show
that rats who are fed 1/2 the normal calories live
longer.

Why should we let rats outlive us?

128

There are a mind-boggling 10,000 food choices available to us every day.

Pat yourself on the back when you make the right choice.

129

Want to order in organic food? Go to your local bookstore or library for tons of catalogues.

130

Skip the alcohol.
It disrupts the good anti-aging nutrients.

131

You don't have to finish everything on your plate, no matter what your mother said.

132

Here's one time Mom was right.

Chew your food at least 30 times.

The more liquid your food, the faster it will be absorbed and the purer the nutrients.

133

Make up "Youth Baskets". Give them to your friends and family as gifts. Include:

    o Cantaloupe
    o Red peppers
    o Carrots
    o Parsley
    o Romaine lettuce
    o Yams
    o Strawberries

134

Remember.

As you age, you need more nutrients and fiber
and a lot less fat and fewer calories.

135

Here's a thought.

Instead of buying that bottle of wine or splurging
on that fatty dessert...write a check for the exact
amount you were going to put into your mouth
and send it to one of the charities feeding the
hungry.

136

Eat natural. The closer your foods are to their
natural state the better.

> Broiled or baked is good.
> Steamed is better.
> Raw is best.

137

This is for all you beer bellies.

The Journal of the American Medical Association tells us that beer slows down your ability to burn off fat. Enough said.

138

Into doggie bags?

Ask for yours **before** dinner...that way you won't be tempted to eat the whole thing.

139

Painless switches to anti-aging foods...and fewer calories to boot!

White bread	to	Whole Wheat
Hamburger	to	Ground Turkey
French Fries	to	Baked Potatoes

140

Eat less, more often.

141

Even the White House is cookin' light.

The old chef is out, the new chef is in.

And the White House chef is on the anti-aging bandwagon.

142

Beta-carotene, as in carrots and cantaloupe may be a sunscreen for your immune system according to *The American Journal of Clinical Nutrition.*

143

Want to know exactly what you are putting into your mouth?

How much fat?
How much vitamin C?
How much vitamin A?
How much vitamin E?
How much calcium?

For a personal diet analysis contact:
The Nutrient Data Research Group
Department of Agriculture
6505 Bellcrest Rd., Hyattsville, MD 20782.

144

Get a water cooler for your home.

145

Eating out tonight? Worst restaurants for anti-aging foods...

> Polish
> Russian
> German
> French
> American
> English
> Italian

Best restaurants for anti-aging foods...

Thai	Indian
Japanese	Seafood
Chinese	Italian

146

Eating out tonight? Stuck? Can't pick the restaurant. O.K.

Italian? Order pasta with pesto sauce, meatless marinara, oil and garlic, or primavera. Going for veal? Stick to piccata, marsala, or scaloppini.

Chinese? Ask for no MSG. Steamed rice and vegetables. Go ahead and have the fortune, but skip the cookie.

Mexican? Black bean soup or gazpacho are good starters. Chicken, shrimp, and rice. Ask for steamed tortillas. No refried beans.

French? Fish, salad, steamed vegetables. Have to have meat? Ask for broiled or grilled.

Pizza? Easy on the cheese. Heavy on the vegetables. Blot with a napkin before you bite.

147

An apple a day **still** makes good sense.

Loads of fiber and new research shows it helps you get a good night's sleep.

148

Yo-yo dieting is aging.

Get to your right weight and stay there.

149

Skeptical about anti-aging nutrients?

Here is some exciting new data from the folks at the U.S. Department of Agriculture's Human Nutrition Research Center on Aging at Tuft's University:

• Vitamins E, B6, and zinc boost immunity.

• Vitamins C, E, and beta-carotene protect against stroke, cancer, heart disease, and cataracts.

• Vitamins B6, B12, folate, calcium, potassium, and soluble fiber reduce the risk of heart disease.

• Vitamins B6, B12, and folate keep you mentally alert.

150

Always live in the raw...raw veggies, that is.

151

Take cooking classes in vegetarian cuisine.

152

Cooking classes don't appeal?

How about these do-it-yourself cookbooks?

Bone Builders™ The Complete Lowfat Cookbook Plus Calcium Health Guide, by Edita Kaye

Butter Busters®Cookbook by Pam Mycoskie

Meatless Dishes in 20 Minutes by Karen Levin

A Feast of Fruit by Elizabeth Riely

Wholesome Harvest by Carol Gelles

Quick Vegetarian Pleasures by Pattina Vitell

The High Road to Health by Wagner & Spade

153

Keeping the youth nutrients in your food.

> o use fresh food whenever possible
> o try to shop every day
> o store food in a cool, dark place
> o if you must mash, peel, or chop, do it
>   right before you serve
> o use minimal amounts of water and oil

154

Feel more tired after breakfast than before?

Need a nap after lunch?

You may be allergic to what you are eating.
Check it out.

155

You are only as young as your arteries.
Don't clog them up.

156

Youth to order.

Check out these suppliers of anti-aging products:

Mrs. Gooch's Natural Food Markets
310-391-5209

Living Foods
510-549-1714

Cheese 'n Stuff
203-233-8281

The Marketplace
505-984-2852

The Good Earth
212-496-1616

Nature's Fresh Northwest
503-234-3008

157

Edita's 10 Commandments To A Long Life

I
Eat enough to maintain a healthy weight.
II
Fat is no more than 20% of your total calories.
III
More vegetables, less meat.
IV
More carbs, less sugar.
V
More fiber.
VI
Less salt.
VII
No alcohol, cigarettes, or drugs.
VIII
Reduce your intake of caffeine.
IX
Take supplements of vitamins and minerals.
X
Eat lots of foods rich in anti-aging nutrients.

158

The food you eat can make you sick.

The food you eat can make you well.

The food you eat can make and keep you young.

159

Make cooking a family affair.

160

Can't eat tons of carrots, cabbage, broccoli, etc...

Drink your anti-aging nutrients.

Invest in a good juicer.

161

Half a "cheat" is better than a whole "cheat".

O.K., so you are going to cheat and eat something that is totally not good for you. Eat half of your junky treat, and throw the rest away. That way you'll only half hate yourself, and do only half the damage.

By the way, you'll still get the "cheat" thrill you crave.

162

Throw an anti-aging pot-luck party.

163

Don't depend on your diet alone to keep you young.

Take supplements.

164

Want great skin...

Vitamin C rebuilds collagen, the underlying base of skin tissue.

165

Having surgery?

o Iron, B12, and folate replace lost blood.

o Vitamin C and vitamin K prevent bruising.

o Zinc helps repair damaged tissues.

o Copper boosts immune function.

o Dietary fibre prevents post-op constipation.

The result?

You are back on your feet faster, better, and younger than ever!

166

Anti-aging tricks for eating out:

o Eat the garnish.
>   Parsley is loaded with vitamin C.
>   Tomato slices ditto.
>   Red pepper slices ditto again.

o Divide your dinner in half on your plate.
>   Eat only the closer half.

o Ask for an extra plate.
>   Slip half your dinner onto it.

o Dressing on the side is still dressing...
>   go for lemon slices instead.

o Skip the menu...too tempting.
>   Order broiled fish, baked potato, salad,
>   steamed veggies.

o Dessert is always fruit.

167

Worst eating out temptation--buffets.

Unless you have remarkable will power, stay far, far away.

168

If you've got time to make a cup of coffee, you've got time to make this anti-aging snack.

Heat a can of low-sodium broth, stir in frozen veggies...voilà...good, hot & healthy!

169

Never let yourself get too hungry.

Eat every three to four hours.

Good choices...complex carbs, fruit and veggies.

170

Best exercise--pushing **away** from the table.

171

Dessert is **always** strawberries, unless you are allergic, then it's cantaloupe.

172

Edita's Daily Anti-Aging Salad

o 1 head romaine lettuce
o 1 red pepper
o 1 cup chopped parsley
o 3 carrots
o 1 lb. broccoli (raw or lightly steamed)

What have you got?
√ 915 mg. calcium
√ 56,150 mg. beta-carotene
√ 1,051 mg. vitamin C
√ a full tummy

173

Make a "to eat" list every day.

As you finish an item, cross it off your list.

Don't add anything new until the next day.

Guaranteed to keep you honest.

174

A good book to have around...*The Wellness Encylopedia of Food and Nutrition* published by the University of California at Berkely. P.O. Box 420422, Palm Coast, Florida 32142.

175

Grow an herb garden with these anti-aging herbs:

Basil	Dill
Oregano	Rosemary
Parsley	Sage

176

Forget cereal. Forget toast.

Have a bowl of pasta for breakfast.

Don't have time to fix it from scratch in the morning? Just make a couple of extra batches when you serve it for dinner and pop it into the microwave for a healthy, filling, low-fat, and satisfying breakfast.

177

Sweet tooth? No problem.

Suck on a butterscotch drop. 25 calories and just a smidgen of fat for all that buttery sweetness.

178

Lots of carrots **do** prevent cataracts and improve your night vision.

179

Make your own bread...great food, great workout.

180

Collect anti-aging recipes. Look for...

> ...low fat shakes and desserts
> ...veggies
> ...dairy products
> ...breads
> ...fish
> ...salads
> ...juices

181

Are you getting enough anti-aging nutrients?
The RDA's may not be enough.

Calcium	1,000 mg.
Vitamin C	1,000 mg.
Vitamin E	400 mg.
Beta-carotene	20,000 I.U.

182

Yo-Yo Weight Loss/Weight Gain could kill you before your time.

Get off the seesaw. Studies show that yo-yo-dieting puts you in a high risk category for heart disease.

183

It it's not there, you won't eat it.

Throw out your anti-aging foods. Start with...

o white bread
o cooking oil
o salt
o soy sauce
o barbecue sauce
o white rice
o sugar coated cereal
o sugar
o sodas

184

Eat some more water to flush out and detox.

These watery foods add H_2O & vital nutrients.

Watermelon	Cantaloupe
Citrus fruits	Lettuce
Cucumber	Low fat yogurt
Spinach	Apples
Peaches	Nectarines
Cabbage	Broccoli

185

Tighten your belt a notch **before** you eat. It works.

186

Calcium is a must for anyone. Here's how to get the 1,000 mg. you need every day.

- o Supplements
- o Sardines with bones
- o Kale, Broccoli, Romaine Lettuce
- o Yogurt
- o Skim Milk (better than whole or partly skimmed)
- o Lowfat cheeses
- o Salmon

187

Don't pig out on anti-aging nutrients.

o Too much fiber causes cramps.

o Too much protein can damage your kidneys.

o Too many beta-carotene foods can turn you yellow.

188

Edita's Personal Anti-Aging Shopping List.

Canola, olive, or avocado oil
Whole grain cereal
Whole wheat bread
Low fat yogurt, fruit or plain
Skim milk
Skinless chicken or turkey, white meat is best
Green, yellow, red fresh vegetables/fruits
Bottled water
Canned/and fresh salmon
Rice cakes
Fig Newtons
Pretzels, no salt
Brown rice
Low salt soup bases
Assorted pasta/no eggs, please
Bagels and/or English muffins
Fruit spread
Herbal teas, assorted

189

Edita's One Day Anti-Aging Mini Fast

Water and carrot juice. Alternate all day. Light dinner heavy on the vegetables.

190

Can't find as many anti-aging products as you would like? Need help? Try? American Botanical Council, P.O. Box 201660, Austin, Texas, 78720.

191

Beef isn't all bad. Lean beef gives you 8 times the vitamin B12 and twice the zinc of poultry. Designer low fat beef by mail. Try...

Coleman Natural Meats, Inc., Denver
1-800-442-8666

Dakota Lean Meats, Inc., Winner, SD
1-800-727-5326

192

Edita's Complete Anti-Aging Food Day

Breakfast:
1 cup bran cereal
1 cup skim milk

Snack:
2 slices whole wheat bread
1 teaspoon fruit spread
1/2 cantaloupe

Lunch:
1 head Romaine
2 red peppers
1 cup parsley
1 tomato
Low fat salad dressing

Snack:
1/2 cantaloupe

Dinner:
1 cup brown rice
1/2 chicken breast broiled
1 lb. broccoli

Bedtime Snack:
2 slices whole wheat bread
1 teaspoon fruit spread

My Little Fountain Of Youth Book

Use It or Lose It

My Little Fountain Of Youth Book

193

Exercise **does** make you younger.

The New York Times reports,"Researchers are finding that moderate exercise cannot only retard the effects of aging, but can actually **reverse** them."

Believe it.

194

Take the pencil test. Can you keep a pencil tucked between your "cheeks" and the tops of your thighs? If it stays, you fail.

Get toned.

195

Dig out your old hula hoop.

196

A daily stroll, according the the Centers for Disease Control, is one of the newest ways to combat aging, (and it's not bad for romance either).

197

Throw an "exercise party".

Forget stuffy, formal, fattening. Offer a....

      o backyard Olympics
      o neighborhood marathon
      o company "walk"

198

Can't afford your own personal trainer? Share.

Try hiring the local highschool coach or gym teacher.Get a couple of Physical Educaton students to put you through your paces.
Last resort...use a video.

199

Who said camp was just for kids?

Outward Bound
212-608-8899

Club Med
212-750-1687

Golf Camp
Roland Stafford Golf School 1-800-447-8894

Kayaking Camp
Otter Bar Kayak School   916-462-4772

Polo Camp
Greenfield Polo and Hunt Club   914-647-3240

Tennis Camp
Gardner's Tennis Ranch   602-948-2100
Saddlebrook Intern'tl Tennis   1-800-729-8383

Triathalon
Tri-Texas Triathalon Camp   210-699-1527

200

Skip a rope.

201

Go dancing.

202

Join the resistance.
    Studies show that resistance training using light weights is great for getting rid of stiff joints. Invest in a pair of 1 or 2 lb. weights and a resistance band and start pumping! Especially good for you youngsters past menopause.

203

Weekend athletes age faster.

Why?

Exercise increases the production of those nasty free radicals that speed up aging. But regular exercise produces antioxidants that offer protection against the free-radical nasties. The warning from the National Institute on Aging is take it easy.

Tip: Don't cram all your exercising into a couple of days. Build slowly to a regular program.

If you pull a "weekend exercise pig-out" take 400 I.U. of vitamin E and load up on vitamin C--both offer antioxidant protection.

204

If you're not walkin' tall, and feelin' fit...
Don't blame your age.
You're just out of shape.

205

Try cross-training between the sheets.

A new position can give a sluggish sex life a real boost. Also, great exercise.

206

Best anti-aging spas....

Spa-Finders Worldwide Catalog of Spas, Fitness Resorts & Retreats. 1-800-255-7727.

207

Walk on the beach. Great positive ions.

208

No time to exercise? Sure there is.

o Walk to work.
o Skip the elevator--take the stairs.
o Park at the f-a-r-t-h-e-s-t entrance to the mall.
o Switch to a push lawnmower.
o Decline the golf cart...carry your clubs.
o Dig a hole...cover it up...dig another one.
o Walk your dog.
o Walk your neighbor's dog.
o Don't walk the dogs together.

209

Sign up for that sport you've always wanted to learn, no matter how exotic, as long as it's fun.

210

Those scientists do it again!

From the researchers at the University of Arkansas, a possible new drug can build muscle while it reduces fat. And firm muscles are youthful muscles. Keep watch for it.

But don't stop exercising.

211

Stand up straight. You'll look younger instantly.

212

Take a walk on the wild side...

Backroads Walking Tours
1-800-245-3874

Country Walkers
802-244-1387

213

Eye exercises for tired, old-looking eyes.

1. Palming.
  Resting your elbows on your desk or a table, close your eyes and cover them lightly with your hands. Great for relieving eyestrain and improving vision. Repeat.

2. Blinking
  Blink rapidly for a few seconds. Close your eyes. Repeat. Blinking lubricates eyes and gives them a necessary break from harsh, aging lights.

214

Need more time for everything?
  Did you know that regular exercise creates more time in your day? You are energized. Alert. You can do more because you are in shape...like staying younger.

215

Hate football? Hate baseball? Try soccer.

United States Amateur Soccer Association
201-861-6277

United States Youth Soccer Association
1-800-4-SOCCER

U.S. Soccer Federation
312-808-9555

216

Buy, rent, or borrow a bike.

217

T.V. Junkies...Go ahead and watch but do it while stepping up and down on a two to four inch box, pedaling a bike, or striding a treadmill.

218

Spend an hour with a six-year old.
Will you get a workout!

Spend an hour with a two-year old...Even better!

219

Can't go the distance? Try listening to easy music
while you exercise. Relaxing music lets you work
out longer. So switch from rock to elevator music.

220

You're still never too old...

- Doc Councilman was 58 when he swam the
  English Channel.
- Ted Williams was 42 when he ended his
  baseball career with a home run.
- Lucille ball was almost 40 when she did the
  first _I Love Lucy_ episode.

221

Just walking is enough to give you major anti-aging benefits.

o Get a good pair of walking shoes.
o Set a good pace. If you can't sing while you walk, you are going too fast.
o Do the "I can't cheat"walk--half an hour away from your home...now you have to walk another half hour to get back. Three times a week, at least.
o Walk with a buddy.
o Join a walking group.
o Bored? Plug in your walkman learn a language, read a book.
o Still bored? Take along a mini tape recorder make a list, dictate a memo, write a book.
o Still bored? You're tough. Develop your own walking tour. Love old houses? Celebrity watching? Great gardens? Find out where they are in your town, and walk to them.

222

Make exercise a family affair.

223

A pot belly can kill you.

Research shows that the roll of fat around your middle puts you at higher risk for cardiovascular disease, hypertension, diabetes, stroke, even sudden death.

Guys, if your waist is bigger than your hips you are getting older faster than you need to.

The same goes for you ladies.

224

Stressed out?
Take a deep breath. Take a walk. Take a break.

225

Give a gift of exercise to someone you love.

226

Aerobics lovers--switch to low impact and save your hearing.

Studies show that high impact aerobics may damage your inner ear and possibly make you deaf prematurely.

227

Yoga, anyone?
Great for relaxation and flexibility.

The American Yoga Association Beginner's Manual
by Alice Christensen.

228

Less may be more.

Workout at 60% of your maximum heart rate for
anti-aging benefits.

229

Use it...you'll have it all much longer.

My Little Fountain Of Youth Book

Age is a State of Mind

My Little Fountain Of Youth Book

230

Age is a state of mind.
You are only as old as you think you are.

231

Surround yourself with symbols for a long life:

Turtles

> They represent long life because many of
> them live to be 130 years old or more.

Cranes

> The Japanese believe cranes live for 1,000
> years and keep company with the gods of
> longevity.

Hares

> South Africans believe hares are the
> keepers of the elixir of life.

Deer

> Koreans believe deer symbolize eternal
> life.

232

Take up music. Musicians live longer...

Toscanini lived to 90.
Bruno Walter lived to 85.
Walter Damrosch lived to 88.
Leopold Stokowski lived to 95.
Andrés Segovia lived to 90.

233

"Smart Drugs" also called cognitive enhancers might boost your brain power and stave off memory loss...a bane of aging.

Interested?
Read *Smart Drugs & Nutrients* by Dean and John Morgenthaler.

234

Say a little prayer. Research shows that religion is a major positive influence on health--and good health means long life.

235

Make friends. People with friends live longer.

236

Set a goal and reach it....

...paint a picture
...run a marathon
...read a book
...take a class
...get a better job
...lose weight
...whatever!

237

Do something for someone who is in worse shape than you.

Selfishness is aging.
Selflessness is anti-aging.

238

Count your blessings.

Don't have any?
 Invent some.

239

Play headgames:
        Do a crossword
        Take up bridge
        Learn chess

240

Believe in the fountain of youth.

241

Get younger with a buddy. Find a friend who wants to get younger and swap anti-aging tips and strategies.

242

Start planning your 100th. birthday party.
If you already are 100,
start planning for 120.

243

Clean out your mental closets.

Get rid of old attitudes.
Throw away old ideas.
Scrap old, unhealthy thoughts, myths and beliefs.

244

Stop saying:

> "I'm too old."
> "You're too old."
> "It's too late."
> "Act your age."

245

There **is** a mind-body anti-aging connection.

246

Pat yourself on the back every day.

247

Pat someone else on the back every day.

248

Go for **IT**. Whatever your personal **IT** might be.

249

Use your imagination. The power of the mind is mighty.

> Picture yourself slim.
> Picture yourself active.
> Picture yourself healthy.
> Picture yourself energetic.
> Picture yourself glowing.
>
> Picture yourself blowing out the candles on your 100th birthday cake.

250

Make a donation to a good cause...one that keeps our earth young and vital.

251

Learn how to program your VCR.

252

Play with toys:

> Crayons
> Leggo's
> Silly Putty
> Pick-up-sticks
> Play-Doh

253

Meditate.

254

Can't meditate? Contemplate your navel.

255

O.K. Seriously, meditation has been linked to longevity for centuries. Find a retreat and go.

256

Smile.

257

Start a private journal.

Write about your goals, your feelings, your hopes, dreams and disappointments. It will be a calming influence.

258

Celebrate every good thing that happens to you, no matter how small.

259

Take a memory improvement course.

260

Be positive.
You are as young as your hope...
     as old as your despair.

261

Whistle a happy tune.

262

Keep a box of "feel goods."
Go through them every time you feel blue.

     o Photos
     o Dried flowers from special dates
     o Old love letters
     o New love letters

263

Never give up on life.

264

Never give in to these reasons for ending it all...

- o Boredom
- o Lack of fun
- o Hopelessness
- o Peer pressure

265

Never stop learning on the job.

266

Find a role model...preferably someone MUCH older than you.

267

Plan something wonderful to look forward to...a great vacation..that college degree...even a fun weekend.

268

These brains never stopped working.

Bertrand Russell, Claude Monet, George Bernard Shaw kept working well in their 80s and 90s.

269

Go to a lecture.
Go to a foreign film.
Go to a museum.
Go to a new restaurant.
Go to an art gallery.
Take in an opera

Break old, dull habits. Stretch that brain.

270

Invite an anti-aging speaker to your office...
Look up Speaker's Bureaus in the Yellow Pages.

271

Never underestimate the rejuvenating power of
laughter.

272

Enjoy every day, and you'll enjoy the weeks,
months and years.

273

Health trumps wealth every time.

274

Get a life.

275

Love yourself.

276

Today is the first day of the rest of your life, make it a long and healthy one.

Words to Get Young By

My Little Fountain Of Youth Book

277

"As you get older, don't slow down. Speed up.
There's less time left."   *Malcolm Forbes*

278

"...what I *really, really, really* want for Christmas
        is just this:

I want to be five years old again for an hour.
I want to laugh and cry a lot.
I want to be picked up and rocked to sleep in
                someone's arms, and carried to bed
                just one more time.
I know what I really want for Christmas.
                I want my childhood back..."

                Robert Fulgham
                *All I Really Need To Know I Learned
                In Kindergarten*

279

"The secret of staying young is to live honestly, eat slowly, and lie about your age." *Lucille Ball*

280

"Everything happens to everybody sooner or later if there is enough time." *George Bernard Shaw*

281

"Our life is frittered away by detail. ....Simplify, simplify." *Henry David Thoreau*

282

"Man does not die--he kills himself." *Seneca*

283

"Age does not protect you from love. But love, to some extent protects you from age."

Jeanne Moreau. French Actress

284

"It's no secret--the people who live long, are those who long to live."   *Anonymous*

285

"Life begins at forty."   *Anonymous*

286

"When he is born, man is soft and weak;
In death he becomes stiff and hard.
The ten thousand creatures and all plants and
        trees
Are supple and soft in life,
But brittle and dry in death.
Truly, to be stiff and hard is the way of death;
To be soft and supple is the way of life.

> *Lao Tze*
> *Quoted in The Tao of Health, Sex &*
> *Longevity*

287

"Do not go gently into that good night,
Old age should burn and rave at close of day;
Rage, rage against the dying of the light."

> *Dylan Thomas*

288

"He was a hundred years of age that day;
He had lived more than the allotted span;
He had carried burdens hard to bear;
He was every inch a man;
'Twas on this birthday that he said
Of worries great and small:
"The things that never happened
Were the biggest of them all"."

Anonymous

289

"For age is opportunity no less
Than youth itself, though in another dress,
And as the evening twilight fades away
The sky is filled with stars, invisible by day."

Henry Wadsworth Longfellow

290

"Longevity is only desireable if it increases the duration of youth, and not that of old age..."

Alexis Carrel

For Women Only

My Little Fountain Of Youth Book

291

"From birth to 18 a girl needs good parents.
From 18 to 35 she needs good looks.
From 35 to 55 she needs a good personality.
From 55 on, she needs cash."

Sophie Tucker

292

Move to Italy. There, women aren't considered interesting or even sexy until they are over 40.

293

Marry a younger....much younger man.

294

Fruit is not just for eating, it's for wearing. Check out these fruit or alpha-hydroxy acid over-the-counter alternatives to Retin-A.

o Alpha Hydrox Face Cream
o BeneFit Glycol
o LaPrairie Age Management Serum
o Eucerin Plus Moisturizing Lotion
o Avon Anew Perfecting Complex
o Estee Lauder Fruition Triple ReActivating
      Complex
o Chanel Formulae Intensive Day Lift Refining
      Complex
o Elizabeth Arden Ceramide Time Complex
      Moisture Cream

295

Work out.

Studies show that as little as 20 minutes of walking three times a week can protect you from aging heart disease and weight gain.

296

Paint your bedroom peach. Better yet, paint your whole house peach.

297

Watch "The Golden Girls."

298

Be a "Golden Girl."

299

Thank heaven you are a woman.

Did you know that women use less oxygen than men, burn energy more slowly, and have a slower metabolic rate than men?

That's terrific news in terms of fighting the aging effects of free radicals associated with oxygen use.

300

Hot flash relief...ginseng available in most health food stores.

301

Your life expectancy is 78. His is 71.

Your best revenge? You'll outlive him.

302

Get mad.

The University of Michigan reports that women who express their anger live longer.

303

"It is sad to grow old, but nice to ripen."
Brigitte Bardot

304

Picture perfect.

Use the powerful technique of visualization to help you select the right anti-aging foods.

Try this exercise: Imagine your stomach as a beautiful, sparkling, clean crystal bowl. Think of it filled with a crisp, fresh, leafy salad or fresh fruit. Wonderful.

Now picture that shimmering bowl sticky, smudged and streaked with gummy pizza, ickky chocolate, smears of lard, all floating in a sea of dark soda. Disgusting.

305

Sunshine as a breast cancer deterrant.

Sunshine may help ward off breast cancer because it helps the body manufacture vitamin D which has been shown to have anticancer properties.

Just ten minutes a day of sun does the trick. Go out, enjoy, but don't forget the sunscreen if you are going to be a sunshine girl for more than 10 minutes.

306

Anti-aging make-up tricks. Not drastic, these small changes can give you a more youthful appearance.

a) Lighten brows.
   Brows that are too dark are aging. Use a little taupe eye shadow on a stiff brow brush, or a light pencil.

b) Use concealer under eyes and in furrow between nose and corners of lips. Pick a shade one tone lighter than your skin.

c) Brighten your blush. Place it high on your cheeks and blend it up into your hairline. It will give your whole face a lift and draw attention away from aging areas.

d) Finish and set makeup with a fat brush dipped in baking powder.

307

Check your skin regularly for signs of skin cancer.

308

Start your own collection of anti-aging articles.

Clip them from magazines and newspapers. Buy a colorful binder and give copies to your friends.

309

Fake a tan. Instead of aging sun try...

o A self tanner. Follow package directions.
o A tinted moisturizer or bronzer.
o Bronzing powder on cheeks, eyelids and forehead.

310

Are you an apple or a pear?

Is your waist the same size as, or bigger than your hips? If the answer is yes, look out. Potbellies increase your risk of heart disease, hypertension, diabetes, stroke and other aging diseases.

311

Get a job. Better yet, get a career.

Researchers at the University of California at San Diego School of Medicine found that career women smoked less, drank less, exercised more, had lower blood pressure and were less likely to get a heart attack.

312

Down in the dumps? Don't feel sexy? Too old? Rent *The Graduate* or *Night of the Iguana* and let these two mature women inspire you.

313

Ever wonder why men appear younger than women as they age?

Could it be that men have been steadily removing dead skin layers every morning as they shave?

Start scrubbing...exfoliate daily with a buff puff.

314

Shades of summer can be aging for your eyes...learn how to shop for the best anti-aging sunglasses. Why? Sunglasses should be coated to protect your eyes from aging ultraviolet light (UV).

Here's what to look for:

   o Look for a tag that reads UV100. These screen out most of the harmful rays. Most sunglasses only screen out about 30% to 40%.

   o Choose glasses that have amber or gold lenses. The closer to the yellow light spectrum the better.

   o Beware of very dark sunglasses without sufficient UV protection. These ultra-dark lenses make your pupils dilate (open wider) and get an even bigger dose of the damaging UV light.

315

Give yourself an anti-aging gift.

Lunch with a friend, an afternoon movie, a facial, a nap.

Be good to yourself.

You're the only "self" you've got.

316

His job may be killing you both.

An intriguing new study shows that if men are in danger of dying on the job, their wives share the risk. Make sure your man takes safety and stress precautions. You'll both live longer.

317

The healthy breast diet.

The less fat the better. No more than 25% of total calories should be from fat...10% is better.

318

Get a custom-made anti-aging jigsaw puzzle. Send your favorite saying, picture, or grouping to
Bit's & Pieces
1-800-JIGSAWS.

319

Take a basil break.

This is one of the healthiest, vitamin rich, anti-aging herbs around. Toss the dry stuff. Grow your own, or buy it fresh and keep it with stems immersed in a glass of water in your fridge. It's good for a week.

320

How much fat is your daily max?

Remember the less the better. This table is a good guide and is based on 25% of your total daily caloric intake as fat.

Total Calories	Grams of fat
1200	33
1400	34
1600	44
1800	50
2000	56
2200	61
2400	67
2600	72
2800	78

321

What's your betacarotene count?

Betacarotene, found in carrots, cantaloupe and other yellow and green leafy veggies is being heralded as a vital nutrient in the prevention of heart disease and certain forms of cancer. Now researchers have found a way to measure just how much betacarotene you have in your system with a simple blood test.

For more information contact
The Nichols Institute,
San Juan Capistrano, California.
714-728-4000.

322

Don't forget to keep the rest of you young...

o Neck   o Hands
o Shoulders   o Feet
o Cleavage   o Legs
o Back

323

"An archaeologist is the best husband any woman can have. The older she gets, the more interested he is in her."   *Agatha Christie*

324

If you can predict your own menopause you'll get a headstart in protecting yourself from such age-related diseases as osteoporosis, heart disease and certain forms of cancer.

How can you tell when the Big M is likely for you?

The longer your cycle between periods and the more children you have, the later your menopause is likely to be.

325

For menopause information try:

(1) Consumer Information Center
      Pueblo, CO 81009
(2) National Women's Health Network
      Washington, D.C. 20005
(3) "A Friend Indeed" Newsletter
      P.O. Box 1710,Champlain, NY 12919

For Men Only

My Little Fountain Of Youth Book

326

Guys, did you know that women make one million more visits to a doctor and live on average, seven years longer?

Does this tell you anything?

327

"Sleep that knits up the ravelled sleeve of care...."

New research from Duke University found that men between the ages of 60 and 72 who didn't exercise regularly had more periods of lighter sleep and were awake more often during the night than men who exercised.

Get moving.

328

Real men wear sunscreen.

329

Married men live longer.

According to a study by the University of California, San Francisco, men between the ages of 45 and 64 who live alone or with a girlfriend or lover, are twice as likely to die within 10 years as men of the same age who live with a wife.

Get that ring!

330

Is your golf game aging you?

Check out the pesticides. If your club isn't using organic pesticides you could develop a rash, fatigue, unexplained headaches, nausea and a depressed immune system. More, your coordination could be off, affecting your game.

Want more info?
Contact the folks at the National Coalition Against The Misuse of Pesticides.
202-543-5450.

331

Know your heart attack risk profile.

o Heart disease runs in your family
o Diagonal crease across your earlobe (no
   kidding)
o High blood pressure
o High cholesterol level
o Little or no regular exercise
o Midthirties baldness
o Beer or potbelly

332

Get rid of hostility. Hostile men die younger.

333

Experts suggest daily anti-aging nutrients:
1,000 mg. vitamin C
400 I.U. vitamin E
20,000 I.U. beta-carotene
1,000 mg. calcium

334

Tall men live longer.

No kidding. Harvard Medical School found that men under 5'7" have a 60% greater chance of getting a heart attack. What can you do, if you can't grow? Eliminate other risk factors.

P.S. The same holds true for women.

335

Losing hair?

Relax. As you get older you'll get hairier...more hair in your ears, nostrils, on your back, and let's not forget those great, intimidating, bushy brows.

336

Have hair, but it's grey?
You are not alone. Men spend $120 million a year to cover their grey.

337

Here's a tip from an Ancient Oriental Philosopher:

"In spring a man may permit himself to ejaculate once every three days, but in summer and autumn he should limit his ejaculations to twice a month. During the cold of winter a man should preserve his semen and avoid ejaculation altogether. A man who follows this guideline will live a long and healthy life." *Liu Ching, Han Dynasty*

338

"After thirty-five a man begins to have thoughts about women; before that age he has feelings."
Austin O'Malley

339

Make money.

Men who feel financially comfortable live longer.

340

Take time to re-think your friendships and connections with others.

  o Go through your rolodex and eliminate as many negative thinkers as possible.

  o Connect with really good friends at least once a month and don't talk business.

  o Make friends with a woman...her insights can be valuable to you.

341

Switch to veggies.

Vegetarian men at age 25 live another 59 years. Meat-eating guys at age 25 live only another 47 years.

342

Get regular check-ups.

343

Stop occasionally and smell the flowers.

344

"Retirement kills more people than old age."

Malcolm Forbes

Age-Proof Your Kids

My Little Fountain Of Youth Book

345

The news on kids isn't so good.

Our kids are getting older, younger.

346

Weigh your kids.

One out of every three kids is overweight.

So what? Fat kids = older, sicker adults.

347

More bad news.

One out of every three kids from kindergarten on, are walking around with super high cholesterol levels making them prime candidates for a younger, old age. Add a cholesterol test to their next physical.

348

Stop telling your kids to finish what's on their plates...unless its part of the fruit or veggie family.

349

Start a "Let's bring back Popeye" club for kids.

350

Teach your kids that love goes with marriage and they should be patient.

351

Teach them to say NO to drugs and alcohol.

25% of American kids say their friends drink and smoke...one of those "friends" could be your kid.

352

Set a good example...always.

353

Kids need anti-aging nutrients too.

Here's how to slip them in so they don't even notice.

• Low fat yogurt fruit shakes

• Turkey burgers

• Fresh spinach or romaine instead of regular lettuce

• Veggie pizza--don't forget to blot each slice before serving

• Parmesan cheese instead of salt on popcorn

• Grated carrots "hidden" in tuna or egg salad

• Fig Newtons and Angel Food Cake for dessert

• Pasta for breakfast

354

Personal tube of their very own sunscreen.

355

Go for a family walk...

> o To the store
> o In the woods
> o To the library
> o To rent a video
> o Wherever.....

356

Give your kids a reward for every healthy thing they do or eat every day.

357

Workout with your kids:

      o Aerobics
      o Yoga
      o Light weights
      o Swimming
      o Sports

358

Kids get stressed too.

Talk to them, <u>really</u> talk to them, every day.

359

Give your kid a massage...end with a tickling session.

360

Give your kid a great big hug.

My Little Fountain Of Youth Book

The Beginning,
Not the End

My Little Fountain Of Youth Book

361

Become an anti-aging guinea pig.

That's right, get in on the ground floor of some very exciting experiments.

Contact The Recruitment Department of the U.S. Department of Agriculture Human Nutrition Center, 711 Washington St., Boston, MA 02111.

362

Start getting younger right now.

> o Order one of the resources in this book.
> o Take a walk around the block.
> o Slap some sunscreen on your face & hands.
> o Eat a carrot.

Just do it!

363

"Live long and prosper."   *Mr. Spock*

364

"Grow old along with me!
The best is yet to be..."   *Robert Browning*

365

Take Edita's Anti-Aging Pledge

"I promise myself that I will take good care of my body and my mind and my spirit, so that all of me is around, intact, and functioning on my next birthday, and the next, and the next, right up to 100-and-something!"

Edita is available to speak to your group or organization.

Edita Kaye
Fountain of Youth Group, Inc.
830-13 A1A North
Ponte Vedra Beach, FL 32082

My Little Fountain Of Youth Book